TE DUE

in the news™

THE TALIBAN IN AFGHANISTAN

Larry Gerber

ROSEN
PUBLISHING®

New York

Published in 2011 by The Rosen Publishing Group, Inc.
29 East 21st Street, New York, NY 10010

Copyright © 2011 by The Rosen Publishing Group, Inc.

First Edition

Library of Congress Cataloging-in-Publication Data

Gerber, Larry, 1946–
The Taliban in Afghanistan / Larry Gerber. — 1st ed.
    p. cm. — (In the news)
Includes bibliographical references and index.
ISBN 978-1-4358-9445-7 (library binding) — ISBN 978-1-4488-1677-4
(pbk.) — ISBN 978-1-4488-1685-9 (6-pack)
1. Taliban—Juvenile literature. 2. Afghanistan—History—1989–2001—
Juvenile literature. 3. Afghanistan—History—2001—Juvenile literature. I.
Title.
DS371.3.G46 2011
958.104'6—dc22

                                                      2009047164

Manufactured in the United States of America

CPSIA Compliance Information: Batch #S10YA: For further information, contact Rosen Publishing, New York, New York, at 1-800-237-9932.

On the cover: Clockwise from top left: An Afghan woman looks through the mesh of her burka; students recite the Qur'an at a madrassa in Pakistan; Taliban fighters.

contents

Land of Warriors

The Taliban seemed to come out of nowhere. In the early 1990s, few Westerners had even heard the name. In less than three years, the Taliban had taken control of Afghanistan, imposing their harsh rules on millions of people. The United States and its allies drove the Taliban from power in 2001 for allowing terrorists to operate from Afghanistan. But the Taliban returned, regaining control of large areas of the country. They would go on to battle the world's strongest armies.

The Taliban is an extremely religious movement of Muslims who enforce their version of Islamic law and tribal customs in areas of Afghanistan and Pakistan. The Taliban ruled Afghanistan from 1996 to 2001. The word *taliban* means "students of Islam," and many members of the Taliban spent their childhood in religious schools. Many were refugees who lost their families and their homes in the wars that have ravaged Afghanistan since 1979.

In Western countries today, the Taliban is despised and feared. The Taliban is condemned for supporting terrorism, denying education to girls, and forcing women to wear head-to-toe burkas. The television news shows videos of mobs burning books and CDs and religious police beating people with sticks. There are reports of the Taliban carrying out executions in sports stadiums, where a crowd is forced to watch.

On the other hand, people in some parts of the world admire the Taliban as a group of religious freedom fighters. But no matter what people think of the Taliban, practically everyone has heard of them.

How could a small group of religious students take over a country? Why do they hate movies, television, music, and seemingly everything about Western culture? What do they have against women? Are they terrorists? Are they freedom fighters? To understand the Taliban, we need to look first at the country of Afghanistan. Its forbidding landscape, its people, their history, and their religion are the forces that shaped the Taliban.

Rough Roads Across Asia

Afghanistan is slightly smaller than the state of Texas. Its mountain ranges, the Pamirs and the Hindu Kush, are higher than any in the United States. They cover the

The Silk Road, pictured here on a fourteenth-century map, has been a trade route between China and Europe since ancient times.

north, east, and central parts of the country. Harsh deserts make up the south and west. Afghanistan has no seacoast.

Afghanistan is one of the world's poorest countries. The harsh landscape and climate make it difficult for farmers to grow food crops, and the country has few natural resources. Afghanistan has several large cities, but most Afghans live in remote villages. Less than 30 percent of Afghans know how to read and write.

Afghanistan's mountains, deserts, and landlocked location have always made it difficult to reach from the outside world. The terrain also makes travel and communication difficult within the country. Afghanistan has no railroad system. Its highways are mostly narrow and bumpy. In winter, it's hard to travel at all.

Despite its isolation, Afghanistan occupies an important place at the crossroads of Asia. Ancient traders traveled the Silk Road on camels, bringing exotic goods from China to the Middle East and Europe. Nowadays, cargo trucks from China, Iran, Pakistan, and other countries in central Asia rattle along its primitive highways.

Afghanistan's poor highway system and rugged terrain shaped the way war is fought there. A small group of determined fighters can control miles of territory. Even in peacetime, accidents, snow, and rockslides may block roads for days. Guerrilla units find it relatively easy to do the same. So do common bandits, who have plagued travelers in Afghanistan for hundreds of years. As we shall see, control of the roads has been important for the Taliban from the very beginning.

Proud People, Strong Traditions

Practically all members of the Taliban are ethnic Pashtuns, which is Afghanistan's largest ethnic group and makes up about 42 percent of its population. Their language is called Pashto. Pashtuns live all over Afghanistan, but their traditional homeland stretches from western Afghanistan across the southern deserts, the eastern mountains, and into Pakistan. The region's main city is Kandahar.

For generations, Pashtuns have lived by an unwritten code of ethics and behavior known as Pashtunwali, or "the Pashtun way." Here are some of its principles:

- Defending personal honor, as well as the honor of family, religion, and culture
- Faith in God

- Hospitality, courtesy, and respect for guests no matter who they are
- Revenge for all wrongs, even verbal insults, no matter how long it takes. This may mean killing the offender or one of his male relatives.
- Asylum and protection for people who seek refuge from their enemies
- Defending their land and property against all intruders
- Defending the honor of women and protecting them from physical harm or insults. This includes strict rules regarding the separation of men and women.
- Letting a council of elders, or *jirga*, make decisions affecting the community

The principles of Pashtunwali may be applied differently in different places. For example, nomadic Pashtuns living in the countryside may be less strict about separation of the sexes than Pashtuns who live in cities.

Many Pashtuns believe that the Taliban has twisted Pashtunwali principles. Even though most Taliban members are ethnic Pashtuns, it's important to remember that many Pashtuns oppose the Taliban.

Tajiks are Afghanistan's second-largest ethnic group. They are historically city dwellers and are often at odds with more conservative Pashtuns. The major cities in the north and west of Afghanistan—Kabul, Mazar-e-Sharif, and Herat—are home to many Tajiks. The Tajiks' culture and history are closely linked to Iran's. Tajiks speak Dari, which is similar to Farsi, the language of Iran. Both Pashto and Dari are the official languages of Afghanistan.

Afghanistan is also home to several smaller minority groups. They include the Hazaras, who were bitterly persecuted under Taliban rule, and the Uzbeks, who speak a language related to Turkish.

A Long History of Warfare

Firearms are widespread in Afghanistan. Shopkeepers in Kabul, the capital, like to display long-barreled muskets used by Pashtun tribesmen against British armies in the 1800s. Teenage security guards hang out on street corners, toting AK-47s. Guns are easy to buy, and marksmanship is a strong tradition among Pashtuns.

War has been a way of life for thousands of years. Alexander the Great led his conquering army into the region more than 2,300 years ago. Arab armies spread the word of the prophet Muhammad to Afghanistan in the seventh century CE. In the Middle Ages, nomadic warriors swept across Asia under Genghis Khan and, later, Tamurlane.

During the 1800s, Russia and Britain wrestled for influence in Afghanistan. The British had an empire in

The AK-47 automatic rifle is a common sight in Afghanistan. Many Afghan boys learn to handle firearms in their early teens.

India, and the Russians had an empire in central Asia. Afghanistan was situated between the two. This conflict was called the Great Game. Between 1839 and 1919, Pashtuns fought three wars against the British. The first war ended after the tribesmen massacred 4,500 British troops and thousands more of their civilian followers. The British invaded again in 1879 and put a friendly Pashtun ruler on the throne after several battles. A brief third war in 1919 ended with independence for Afghanistan under a Pashtun king.

A border drawn by the British during this time created problems. Afghanistan's eastern border still runs through the ancient Pashtun homeland, separating millions of Pashtuns in Pakistan from those in Afghanistan.

Afghanistan and the Soviet Union

In 1917, shortly before Afghanistan gained its independence, a revolution occurred in Russia. The aristocratic rulers that had controlled Russia were overthrown, and a

Refugees of a Wrecked Society

The Soviet invasion wiped out the last traces of popular respect for the government in Kabul. In addition, it effectively brought an end to national unity. Afghans everywhere opposed both the invaders and the government.

Although the mujahideen fought the Soviets, they were never a united force. Instead, they were composed of separate groups that followed local commanders. These local commanders operated independently of one another, and many mistrusted each other. The mujahideen's fragmented leadership meant the Soviets had to fight everywhere, making it impossible to crush the resistance. Small groups of guerrilla fighters would attack and then disappear into the mountains, where tanks and large troop formations could not follow.

The Soviets stepped up their use of helicopters and planes. The United States responded by sending the mujahideen antiaircraft rockets. Saudi Arabia was another major supporter of the rebels. Rather than

Mujahideen fighters with an antiaircraft gun watch for Soviet planes and helicopters. The guerillas fought the Soviets for ten years and eventually drove them out of Afghanistan.

sending aid directly, Americans and Saudis moved supplies through Pakistan. Pakistani intelligence officers decided how many weapons each mujahideen group would get.

Young men from Islamic countries came to Afghanistan to fight in what they saw as a holy war. One of these young men was a wealthy Saudi Arabian named Osama bin Laden.

The fighting dragged on and became increasingly bloody. At the height of the war, the Soviet Union had approximately one hundred thousand troops in Afghanistan. They bombed and rocketed villages, trying to hit the elusive mujahideen. The Soviets also hid many land mines throughout Afghanistan. These land mines were especially dangerous for children because many of them looked like toys.

The fighting destroyed irrigation systems needed to grow crops and left Afghanistan in ruins. Millions of villagers had to flee their homes. Unknown thousands were killed. The invasion was also a disaster for the Soviet Union. By 1989, its Communist leaders realized they could not defeat the mujahideen. Fifteen thousand

Soviet soldiers had been killed. The demoralized invaders went home. Two years later, the Soviet Union fell apart.

Civil War

Afghanistan's nightmare continued. The Soviet-backed national government kept fighting the mujahideen, but it was finally overthrown in 1992 after the Soviet Union collapsed. The mujahideen commanders, unable to agree on a new government, soon began fighting among themselves.

In some ways, this chaotic civil war was worse than the fight against the Soviets. Afghans were not only fighting each other, but they also had access to tons of weapons and military supplies left behind by the Soviets.

Kabul, the capital, came under the control of forces led by Ahmad Shah Massoud. A Tajik from northern Afghanistan, Massoud was regarded as a hero for his resistance to the Soviets. He was allied with Uzbek fighters and others from northern Afghanistan.

They were soon attacked by a Pashtun leader named Gulbuddin Hekmatyar. In 1993, Hekmatyar's men shelled and rocketed the capital, killing civilians without mercy. All over the country, the situation kept worsening. Militia leaders fought and switched sides. Petty warlords in southern Afghanistan began kidnapping, robbing, and seizing people's homes. Ordinary citizens were sick of war and wanted only peace. The former mujahideen commanders became hated and feared.

Millions of refugees wanted to come back to Afghanistan but were afraid to. Most of these people were stuck in huge refugee camps that had grown up across the border in Pakistan. They lived in tents, receiving food and shelter from charity groups.

Students of Islam

Saudi-funded Islamic charities supported schools for the refugees. These madrassas, or schools of the Islamic religion, provided the only educational opportunity for many refugee boys. The madrassas also provided students with meals and a place to sleep.

Madrassa schools, which have a long tradition in Islamic countries, concentrate on religious studies. But many madrassas also teach other subjects and prepare students for life in an Islamic society.

In the madrassas that offered a place to the young Taliban, teachers emphasized reading so students could study the Qur'an, the holy book of Islam. These teachers believed that most other studies were unnecessary. Some teachers knew no subjects other than the Qur'an.

Boys study the Qur'an at a madrassa in Pakistan. Many madrassa students joined the Taliban in order to end the civil war and bring Islamic law to Afghanistan.

Most Saudi-funded madrassas taught the strict version of Islam practiced in Saudi Arabia. Females were excluded from the classroom. Many Taliban grew up apart from their mothers or sisters, in a world with little or no female influence. Those who had been born in refugee camps had little knowledge of normal society in Afghanistan.

Angry at the destruction of their homeland and disgusted by the abuses of the militia warlords, groups of students and teachers began talking about joining forces and reuniting Afghanistan under the banner of Islam. They believed that God was on their side.

Muhammad and What He Taught

Practically all Afghans are Muslims. The Muslim religion is called Islam, which means "submission." Muslims believe that the word of God was given to the prophet Muhammad, who was born in 570 CE in Mecca, a city located in present-day Saudi Arabia. After his death in 632, Muhammad's divine revelations were collected and written down in a book known as the Qur'an. His followers carried Islam across much of Asia and North Africa.

The foundations of the Islamic faith are known as the Five Pillars of Islam. Muslims may disagree on various aspects of Islam, but these five beliefs are fundamental for all:

- The profession of faith: "There is no God but God, and Muhammad is his messenger." Muslims use the Arabic name Allah for God. They believe that this god is the same god worshipped by Jews and Christians.
- Prayer: Muslims focus their mind on God through prayer five times every day.
- Charity: Muslims are required to give alms to the poor.

This picture from the sixteenth century CE depicts an angel delivering the word of God to the prophet Muhammad.

- Ramadan: During one month each year, Muslims fast from sunup to sundown.
- Pilgrimage: At least once in a lifetime, Muslims are expected to make a pilgrimage, or hajj, to the holy city of Mecca.

Another important Islamic principle widely misunderstood in the West is jihad. It may mean an armed struggle on behalf of Islam, and Taliban fighters often refer to themselves as jihadis. But jihad also means a person's spiritual struggle to do the right thing. Muhammad gave more importance to the spiritual meaning.

Multiple marriages are allowed for men in Islam, but not for women. Muhammad's first convert was a woman—his wife Khadija. After her death, Muhammad married several times. Islamic law cites several other instances when men and women should be treated differently. However, Muhammad basically taught that all believers are equal and deserve respect regardless of their gender.

There are about 1.3 billion Muslims in the world. They can be found in practically every country, in the poorest areas of the world as well as in the richest. Islam is interpreted in different ways in different places. Some Muslims are tolerant of other religions. Others are strict in their beliefs and intolerant of others. There are two major denominations of Islam: Sunni and Shiite. The Taliban is predominantly Sunni.

The Taliban Comes Together

The early Taliban saw enemies on all sides. They were secretive and mistrustful of outsiders. We know that, in 1994, madrassa students and teachers began gathering in Kandahar around a mullah, or village religious leader, named Omar. Mullah Omar had lost an eye fighting against the Soviet-backed government. However, he was respected more for his religious faith than his military leadership.

Mullah Omar was named Taliban leader by hundreds of Pashtun mullahs who met in Kandahar in 1996. The city was closed to foreigners. Mullah Omar appeared on a rooftop wearing the cloak of the prophet Muhammad, a holy relic kept in a Kandahar shrine. The mullahs in the courtyard below hailed him as "Commander of the Faithful." It meant that they viewed Mullah Omar as leader of Islam's warriors and of Afghanistan. The meeting ended with a declaration of holy war against the national government in Kabul.

Mullah Omar was chosen after the mullahs failed to agree on how Afghanistan should be governed. Should it tolerate modern ideas and other cultures? Mullah Omar and his followers believed not. They believed that their version of Islam was the true religion as practiced in the time of Muhammad, 1,400 years ago. They would make it the law of Afghanistan.

MERIDIAN MIDDLE SCHOOL
2195 Brandywyn Lane
Buffalo Grove, IL 60089

Rise of the Taliban

3

Oppressed by war and crime, many Afghans considered the early Taliban to be heroes who fought the rich to protect the poor. In 1994, stories quickly spread about how the Taliban rescued kidnapped children from vicious militia leaders in the Kandahar area.

Powerful transportation companies in Pakistan were frustrated by the many militias. The former mujahideen were blocking roads across southern Afghanistan, demanding payment from truckers. Convoys were often stopped dozens of times a day by different groups only a few miles apart. Pakistani shippers gave a donation to Mullah Omar and promised him more payments if he could clean up the situation.

In October 1994, about two hundred Taliban from madrassas in Pakistan and Kandahar attacked a border post controlled by the warlord Gulbuddin Hekmatyar and drove off his men. The Taliban then captured a nearby arms dump, taking thousands of AK-47s, artillery pieces, ammunition, and vehicles.

The following month, the Taliban freed a convoy that had been captured by militias near Kandahar. They shot a local commander and hung his body from a tank barrel as an example to others.

The Taliban seized the city of Kandahar that same night, capturing tanks and aircraft. More than two thousand militiamen joined the Taliban. Within three months, the Taliban became a national force, capturing twelve of Afghanistan's thirty-one provinces. From their stronghold of Kandahar, they moved toward Kabul and Herat. Small-unit Pashtun commanders often accepted bribes to surrender. Money for the Taliban was now coming in from Saudi Arabia, Pakistan's intelligence service, Pakistani truckers and, more and more, from the opium trade.

On the road to Herat, the young fighters were joined by Pakistani journalist Ahmed Rashid, one of the few reporters who covered the early years of the Taliban. They told Rashid that twenty thousand Afghans had left refugee camps in Pakistan to join Mullah Omar. Thousands more Pashtuns had joined in Afghanistan. They were eager to bring the whole country under Taliban-style Islamic law.

Winning Control

The Taliban now faced Afghanistan's strongest militia commanders. Ahmad Shah Massoud, commander of Tajik forces in Kabul, drove the Taliban away from the

Tajik commander Ahmad Shah Massoud was one of the main resistance leaders against the Soviets. He later battled the Taliban but was assassinated in 2001.

capital in March 1995. His veterans of the Soviet war were more experienced than the young Taliban fighters, who suffered their first defeat.

Ismail Khan, the most experienced of all the anti-Soviet commanders, also drove the Taliban back from the western city of Herat. The Taliban suffered heavy casualties. Many were left to die in the desert without medical help.

Ismail Khan controlled the roads into Iran. He was unpopular with truckers and drug shippers because of the high tolls he charged. The transporters continued to support the Taliban. Pakistan and Saudi Arabia also helped the Taliban rebuild, supplying them with fresh arms, ammunition, and vehicles. More volunteers came from Pakistan. Taliban fighters loaded into new Japanese pickups and mounted another attack on Herat. The city fell to the Taliban in September 1995. Ismail Khan fled into nearby Iran.

Herat is an ancient center of Persian culture. Most of its people speak Dari. The Taliban occupied Herat like foreign conquerors. Pashtun speakers from Kandahar refused to let local people take any part in the adminis-tration. Schools for both boys and girls had flourished under Ismail Khan's rule. The Taliban closed the schools and restricted girls and women to their homes.

The Taliban victory alarmed Iran, partly because of religious differences. Most Iranians are Shiite Muslims, highly suspicious of the Sunni Taliban. The Taliban's persecution of Shiites in Afghanistan later prompted Iran to denounce the Taliban government. In 1998, the Taliban killing of several Iranian diplomats in Mazar-e-Sharif nearly led to war.

Massacres in the North

The civil war grew more vicious as the months passed. The Taliban repeatedly bombed and rocketed Kabul, killing and injuring hundreds of civilians. The key city of Jalalabad fell to the Taliban in September 1996, and later that same month, the Taliban took control of Kabul. Fighting around the capital and Baghram, the nearby air base, continued for nearly three years.

Most of Afghanistan's people were now under Taliban control. However, the country's richest farms and indus-tries are in the North, and the northern Tajik, Uzbek, and Hazara militias would not surrender them without a fight.

Despite years of war, the beautiful city of Mazar-e-Sharif was mostly untouched. Its people were among

Taliban fighters outside Kabul. Afghanistan's capital fell to the Taliban in 1996 after fighting that caused widespread death and destruction.

the most educated and most liberal in Afghanistan. When 2,500 Taliban troops rolled into the city in their pickups in May 1997, disaster soon followed. The Taliban closed girls' schools and declared Islamic law. Uzbek and Hazara troops thought they would be sharing power with the Taliban, but the Taliban began trying to disarm them. Fighting broke out. The population rose up against the Taliban.

The Taliban fighters did not know the city. They found themselves trapped in a maze of confusing streets and alleys. Some six hundred Taliban were killed and approximately one thousand were captured. The casualties included some of the best Taliban fighters as well as military and political leaders.

Thousands more Taliban fighters were killed in the following weeks as alliance forces recaptured areas between Kabul and Mazar-e-Sharif. It was the worst Taliban defeat ever. The bodies of thousands of Taliban prisoners were later found in mass graves. An Uzbek general was accused of the murders, but no one was actually charged with the crime.

The Taliban took revenge in August 1998. They again swept northward, defeating Uzbek and Hazara militias. Again, they drove their pickups through Mazar-e-Sharif's narrow streets. This time men, women, and children were gunned down. Even goats and donkeys were killed. Contrary to Islamic law, which demands immediate burial, the bodies were left in the streets for days.

The UN estimated that approximately five thousand to six thousand people died in these attacks. Shiite Hazaras were especially persecuted by the Taliban. The main Hazara province is Bamian, in central Afghanistan. The Taliban blocked roads into the province, attempting to starve its people. They kidnapped hundreds of Hazara women and massacred the inhabitants of several villages. By the time Bamian province fell to the Taliban, however, the international community was enraged by the earlier atrocities. Mullah Omar warned the Taliban troops not to commit any more mass killings.

Lion of the Panjshir: Massoud's Resistance

Ahmed Shah Massoud was the best-known leader of the anti-Taliban forces that came to be known in the West as the Northern Alliance. His Tajik forces had defeated the Soviets time after time in their stronghold, the Panjshir Valley. Massoud became known as the Lion of the Panjshir.

According to American journalist Steve Coll, Massoud was visited in 1996 by an American CIA official. Massoud was then in Kabul, serving as defense minister in the government. The Americans had supported Massoud during the Soviet war, but now Massoud felt he had been abandoned. After the defeat of the Soviets, he believed, America had lost interest in Afghanistan. Massoud promised to help the CIA track down the terrorist Osama bin Laden, who had declared war on the United States. However, Massoud was worried that the United States did not understand what was going on in Afghanistan and did not realize how dangerous the Taliban was.

Just a few days after the meeting, the Taliban entered Kabul. Massoud retreated to continue fighting in the north.

Kabul Falls to the Taliban

Years of fighting had reduced much of Afghanistan's capital to rubble. Thousands had left the city, but Kabul was still filled with homeless people who had fled the warfare in the country-side. Tajiks, Uzbeks, Hazaras, and Pashtuns had battled in the streets and fired rockets and artillery from the mountains around the city. Thousands of civilians had been killed or injured.

Women and children try to find safety during fighting near Kabul. Millions have been forced to flee their homes during the years of warfare in Afghanistan.

When the Taliban took Kabul on September 26, their first act was to hang former president Najibullah, who had ruled under the Soviets. He was taken from his hiding place, beaten, mutilated, and shot. The Taliban hung his body from a traffic signal in downtown Kabul. Cigarettes and money were placed in his hands as signs of "corruption." Crowds of people saw the body, which was left hanging as a symbolic act. Many people who had thought of the Taliban as liberators were shocked by this show of brutality.

The Taliban in Power

4

The Taliban quickly began to impose its harsh version of Islamic law. Modern customs and foreign styles were outlawed. No girls over age eight were allowed to go to school. Women were not allowed to have jobs, except for a few female doctors and nurses working in women-only hospitals. Strict rules applied to men as well, and the Taliban's "religious police" became dreaded for their brutal punishments.

Taliban Rules and the "Religious Police"

Whenever they appeared in public, women had to wear a burka. The long, loose garments cover the wearer from head to foot. The area around the eyes is made of mesh fabric, but it is still difficult to see through. Women wear their normal clothes under the burka. Garments like the burka were common throughout much of Asia even before the time of Muhammad. The Prophet urged his followers to dress modestly, but many Muslims say nothing in their religion requires anything so extreme.

Women were forbidden to step outside their homes without the accompaniment of a male relative. Women could not to talk to any males, such as store clerks, who weren't relatives. They could not be photographed or shown in pictures. They could not wear bright colors, makeup, or jewelry. House windows were painted so women could not be seen from the outside. Women were not permitted to laugh in public. The Taliban even demanded that women wear soft-soled shoes that would make no noise when they walked.

The rules laid down by the Taliban affected everyone. Music, movies, television, and video were prohibited. The Internet was banned. People with "non-Islamic" names had to change them. Men and boys had to have short haircuts, and men were required to grow full beards. Kite flying, chess, and other popular pastimes were outlawed. Boys had to wear turbans to school. No pictures of any kind could be hung in shops or hotel rooms.

Groups of "religious police" patrolled cities and villages to enforce the rules. People found in shops during prayer time could be imprisoned. Both men and women could be beaten for a number of offenses. Other penalties were even worse. Criminals convicted in Taliban courts had limbs amputated. Unmarried lovers could be stoned

Even before the Taliban came, many Afghan women wore burkas. However, the Taliban forced all women to wear them and punished those who didn't.

to death. On several occasions, Taliban police forced men and boys into stadiums that had once been used for soccer games and made them watch executions.

Most of the foreign aid workers and journalists remaining in Afghanistan were concentrated in Kabul, the country's capital. When Kabul fell to the Taliban, the world began to hear firsthand accounts of what was happening in Afghanistan. Many people outside of Afghanistan were disgusted by the practices of the Taliban government. But the Taliban cared little for what others thought. They believed they were carrying out the will of God. Negative press reports, and the foreign outcry that followed them, made the Taliban even more suspicious of the few foreigners working in Afghanistan.

Throughout its modern history, Afghanistan has depended heavily on foreign aid. Nongovernmental organizations (NGOs) build and run schools, health services, highways, water systems, and dozens of other services that Afghanistan cannot afford on its own. Several UN organizations and other aid agencies felt threatened by the Taliban and began leaving Afghanistan. Groups helping women found it impossible to carry out their work. The departure of these NGOs made life harder for all of the Afghans who depended on their services.

The United States and other countries publicly condemned the Taliban. Only Pakistan, Saudi Arabia, and the United Arab Emirates recognized the Taliban as the official government of Afghanistan.

A War on Culture

The Taliban's religious warriors did not only oppose Western culture. They attacked Afghan culture as well. The most striking example occurred in Bamian province, homeland of the persecuted Hazaras.

An ancient statue of Buddha towers above two people sitting on its right foot. This picture was taken before the Taliban destroyed the statue and another like it.

Two huge statues of Buddha had been carved into rock cliffs about 1,500 years ago, before Islam came to Afghanistan. The monuments, looking over a beautiful valley, were cultural and historical treasures. In 1998, Taliban vandals attacked the statues with dynamite and rockets but didn't destroy them. In 2001, Mullah Omar declared the statues offensive to Islam. They were blasted to rubble. People around the world were outraged.

The destruction of the Buddhas was only a part of the Taliban's war on culture. Taliban fanatics rampaged through the country's museums, destroying countless smaller treasures. The Taliban claimed the museum pieces violated Islamic laws against idol worship.

Afghanistan has vast fields of poppies that produce opium, the base material used to make heroin. The militia warlords had used drug money to finance their operations, and the Taliban had done the same. Once the

Taliban became established, however, Mullah Omar declared that the drug trade violated Islamic law. All drugs were forbidden. The Taliban forced farmers to destroy their poppy crops and stamped out the opium trade.

Haven for Terror

Osama bin Laden, believed to be the seventeenth son of a Saudi Arabian millionaire, first came to Afghanistan during the 1980s to fight the Soviets. He was welcomed by the mujahideen, and some analysts believe he even received training from the CIA during this time. Bin Laden established an organization to recruit young men around the world and buy equipment for the war against the Soviets.

Osama bin Laden was wanted by U.S. authorities even before the terrorist attacks of September 11, 2001. The Taliban gave him asylum in Afghanistan.

After the Soviets were defeated, bin Laden went home to Saudi Arabia, but he was expelled from the country for his antigovernment activity. He went to

Sudan, in Africa, but was also expelled from there. Now hunted by U.S. authorities, he returned to the only country offering safety: Afghanistan.

Bin Laden proclaimed holy war against the United States and called for the killing of Americans and Jews. Using his inherited wealth, he built a terrorist organization called Al Qaeda, or "the Base." He was accused of plotting several terrorist attacks, including deadly 1998 bombings at U.S. embassies in Kenya and Tanzania.

In 1998, the United States launched a rocket attack against his suspected base in Afghanistan. Several people were killed, but not bin Laden. The Taliban protested the attack. Over the years, the U.S. government kept urging Afghanistan to expel or hand over bin Laden, but the Taliban refused. Mullah Omar said bin Laden could not be harmed because he was a guest.

The Catastrophes of 2001

By 2001, the Taliban controlled practically all of Afghanistan. Only Ahmad Shah Massoud held out against them, secure in his northern stronghold. On September 9, Massoud welcomed two television interviewers into his office. As they prepared for their "interview," they set off a bomb, killing themselves and Massoud. Al Qaeda was believed to be behind the assassination.

Just two days later, hijackers flew U.S. airliners into the World Trade Center in New York City and into the Pentagon, the military headquarters of the United States, outside of Washington, D.C. The World Trade towers collapsed in smoke and rubble. A fourth hijacked airliner crashed in Pennsylvania. In all, nearly three thousand people were killed in the attacks. Millions watched, horrified, as the disasters were broadcast on live television.

Again, the United States demanded that the Taliban surrender bin Laden. Again, the Taliban refused. Americans were enraged—how could any government harbor such a criminal? The Taliban believed it was sticking to the Pastunwali tradition of asylum and protection. But as it had done in many other cases, the Taliban now carried tradition to the extreme.

Many believe that Al Qaeda plotted the killing of Massoud, as well as the attacks on the United States. A connection between these two events has never been proven, especially since all the attackers were killed and could not be questioned. But it seems likely that Al Qaeda decided to get rid of its strongest enemy in Afghanistan before launching the 9/11 attacks. Massoud was a master guerrilla general. If he had lived, many people speculate that he could have helped put an end to the Taliban and damaged Al Qaeda—especially with the full backing of an angry United States.

The World Reacts

5

The day after the September 11, 2001, attacks, U.S. president George W. Bush announced that the United States would wage "war on terrorism" and anyone who helped terrorists. Most of the planes' hijackers were Saudi Arabian citizens. The rest were from other Arab countries. None of them was Afghan. But Osama bin Laden was in Afghanistan, and the United States had run out of patience with the country's Taliban rulers.

Driving Out the Taliban

American planes and ships were soon moving into position to strike targets in Afghanistan. The U.S. military also made an important decision about how the war would be fought, at least in the early stages: troops on the ground would work closely with Northern Alliance forces. These included the fighters who had followed Ahmad Shah Massoud and others who still opposed the Taliban. At this point, the main job of American ground troops would be to guide the U.S. air strikes.

On October 7, 2001, the United States began attacking Taliban and Al Qaeda targets with bombs and missiles. The air strikes quickly destroyed Taliban communications and drove many Taliban fighters into hiding. At this point America did not have many soldiers on the ground, and U.S. air power was not enough to capture Osama bin Laden.

By late November 2001, bin Laden was believed to be hiding in a rugged mountain area near the border with Pakistan. American forces blasted the area with bombs and missiles. However, U.S. forces did not attack on the ground. Instead, they called on their Afghan allies to surround the area. Bin Laden escaped. Afghans involved in the operation said later that local forces had been paid to guard the escape routes. To escape, bin Laden simply paid the guards more money and walked across the border.

American forces soon discovered that their Afghan allies could be a problem in other ways. Some were militia commanders known for their cruelty and criminal activity. They were still distrusted by many Afghans and by each other. Others had made their money from drug trafficking.

Foreign countries sent troops to help the U.S. forces. They included Canada, France, Germany, and the United

Planes launched from U.S. aircraft carriers struck Al Qaeda terrorist camps in Afghanistan and helped drive the Taliban from power.

Kingdom. These combined forces were named the International Security Assistance Force (ISAF). Russia and other countries of the former Soviet Union agreed to let U.S. forces set up bases or cross their territory. Saudi Arabia and the United Arab Emirates broke off diplomatic relations with the Taliban government. Only Pakistan remained friendly.

The Taliban left Kabul in mid-November. By the end of the month, the allies controlled most of Afghanistan.

Some Taliban kept fighting around Kandahar, but they began to surrender after a unit of 1,200 U.S. Marines deployed near the city. These Marines were the biggest American unit on the ground so far.

Many captured Taliban and suspected Al Qaeda members were sent to U.S. prisons for questioning. Prisoners in Kunduz, northern Afghanistan, managed to get hold of weapons and stage an uprising. Hundreds of them were killed, along with

Taliban and Al Qaeda suspects were imprisoned and interrogated at Guantanamo Bay, Cuba, and other prisons. Their treatment led to violent protests in Afghanistan.

about forty allied troops and one CIA agent, who was thought to be the first American killed in the war. The revolt was finally stopped by a U.S. air strike.

Some prisoners captured in Afghanistan were held for years. Their treatment by U.S. authorities would cause widespread resentment and violent protests in the future.

Thousands of Taliban members, including Mullah Omar, fled into Pakistan. Others hid inside Afghanistan. In the following months, they carried out occasional attacks on U.S. and allied forces.

The U.S.-Led Occupation

In late 2001, anti-Taliban Afghan leaders met in Germany to form an interim government headed by Hamid Karzai, a Pashtun. Many Americans believed that the Taliban had been defeated. In May 2003, the U.S. defense secretary said that major combat was over and Afghanistan could focus on rebuilding.

But the Taliban continued to attack. Whenever a large group of Taliban fighters gathered, the United States would try to destroy them with an air strike. But small groups would come out of hiding to fire on Afghan police posts or ISAF bases and supply convoys. Aid workers were killed and government buildings were bombed. The Taliban often used weapons and explosives that had been hidden from the foreign troops. The Taliban remained strongest in the south, where guerrillas battled units of the new national army of Afghanistan. In December 2003, U.S. troops launched a major ground attack on the guerrillas.

A special legislative council adopted a new constitution for Afghanistan in 2004. Hamid Karzai was elected president. However, elections for a national assembly were postponed until 2005 because of security concerns.

Neither the new government nor the U.S.-led military forces seemed able to bring stability. Part of the problem was that people mistrusted the new government. It included militia leaders who were suspected of mass killings and other crimes during the civil war.

These warlords and their followers had returned to the areas they controlled in the days before the Taliban. People were soon complaining again of militia abuses. Neither the new Afghan government nor the U.S.-led military forces were able to control corruption and drug smuggling, especially in remote areas. In many areas, the

Workers count votes after the presidential election of 2004. Hamid Karzai was elected president, but his government failed to stop violence and corruption.

militiamen became more feared than the Taliban. The militias sometimes fought allied troops.

Islamic fanatics also attacked women who tried to work and girls who went to school. In some cases the attackers were members of the Taliban, and in some cases they were not. To make things even more confusing, some criminals wore police uniforms while robbing and kidnapping people. The police, who were poorly paid, sometimes accepted bribes to ignore crimes. And in some cases, the criminals were actually members of the police force. People didn't know whom to trust. Foreign governments spent millions of dollars to train professional police, and there were many honest policemen. But improvement was slow.

The Afghan national army also had problems. Many of the new Afghan soldiers were reluctant to fight the Taliban. Some of them remained more loyal to their family and tribal leaders than to the new national government. Allied commanders said there simply weren't enough men in the Afghan army. Soldiers from the United States and Britain complained that some Afghan soldiers couldn't fight because they were using hashish.

Americans were also distracted by another war. The administration of President George W. Bush claimed that Iraq's dictator, Saddam Hussein, was preparing nuclear weapons and other weapons of mass destruction. In 2003, Bush ordered an invasion of Iraq and persuaded many of America's foreign allies to join. Hussein's regime was quickly defeated, but no weapons of mass destruction were found. American troops in Iraq became involved in a brutal civil war. By the end of 2003, the United States had about 130,000 troops in Iraq, compared with only ten thousand in Afghanistan.

Taliban attacks became more frequent and more serious. The Taliban took control of entire districts in the rugged Pakistan border region. Taliban fighters were sometimes aided by their Pashtun relatives and friends in Pakistan and by Pakistan's Islamic political parties. The winding border with Pakistan was no barrier to anyone

Afghan girls work in a poppy field. After 2001, Afghan poppies became the world's main source of opium and a major source of income for the Taliban.

who knew the mountain passes and trails. Taliban units could plan attacks in Pakistan and cross the border to carry them out. Then they could return to Pakistan to escape U.S. and Afghan government forces.

During the U.S. occupation, farmers again began growing opium poppies. The Taliban had forbidden the crops during their rule. But now that it was out of power and needed money, the Taliban began taxing poppy growers. Opium became an important source of income for the Taliban.

6 Return of the Taliban

Just a few years after the U.S. invasion, the Taliban was back in force. Many of its battle tactics were the same as those of the mujahideen a generation earlier. Taliban fighters attacked from strong points in the mountains and deserts. They often attacked at night, which made it easier for them to escape.

Western armies faced many of the same problems that had plagued the Soviets. They needed tons of supplies, which had to be moved along the country's primitive roads. Convoys frequently came under Taliban attack. U.S. infantrymen hunting for the Taliban were burdened with the heavy equipment and drinking water they had to carry.

The Taliban had also adopted new tactics. They learned to anticipate their enemies' movements. Cell phones, unknown during the Soviet war, were now commonplace. They could be used not only for communication but also for setting off explosives by remote control. The Taliban learned to make bombs out of artillery shells and other material. Allied forces had to be on constant watch for hidden improvised explosive devices (IEDs).

An increasing number of Taliban fighters became willing to die as suicide bombers. During the earlier wars, suicide bombing was fairly rare in Afghanistan. Many Afghans regard it as dishonorable and contrary to Islamic law. As more and more foreigners came to fight with the Taliban, however, suicide bombing became more common.

A U.S. Marine and an Afghan soldier are covered with dust after a Taliban mine explodes during a battle in 2009.

Many of the newcomers in Afghanistan were Iraqis who arrived during the U.S. occupation of Iraq. Other newcomers included Islamic extremists from countries such as Pakistan, the central Asian republics, and Chechnya, which had been a part of the former Soviet Union.

The Taliban also began enlisting part-time fighters. Young Afghans with no jobs could earn money by carrying out Taliban missions such as attacking police posts. Workers in Afghanistan make an average of only $50 a month, and the Taliban would pay twice that or more. The hired fighters could return their weapons at the end of the job and go back to their villages, where it was nearly impossible for foreign troops to find them. Since jobs were so scarce, some experts believed that part-timers fighting for money eventually made up a majority of the Taliban's fighters.

People who didn't sympathize with the Taliban were kept in line by threats and violence. Hidden radio transmitters told people how to behave and broadcast the Taliban version of the news. "Night letters" were another means of intimidation. These were mimeographed sheets posted at mosques or on mud-brick village walls that warned of Taliban punishments for anyone who gave information to allied soldiers. The Taliban threatened to chop off people's fingers if they voted in elections. These threats were often carried out.

The "New" Taliban

As the years passed, Taliban leaders learned the value of public opinion and became less secretive. They began trying to influence people by persuasion as well as by threats and force. Many Afghans listened because they mistrusted outsiders, and the Taliban, for all its faults, was an Afghan organization. U.S. air strikes of Taliban targets often killed civilians, including women and children. This angered many Afghans and made them more willing to accept the Taliban. Imprisonment of Afghans by U.S.

authorities also upset many people. In addition, few Westerners spoke Pashtun, Dari, or the other Afghan languages. Few Afghans speak anything but their native language. So the Taliban also enjoyed a language advantage in the battle for people's hearts and minds.

The Taliban began to care about foreign opinion. Spokesmen were chosen to talk with reporters. Journalists were allowed to visit Taliban units and even watch them stage attacks. Guerrilla fighters, speaking through interpreters, would tell why they opposed the Americans and the government. Knowing that Westerners were reluctant to get bogged down in an endless war, Taliban guerrillas often told reporters that they were willing to fight for years.

In May 2009, Taliban leaders published a code of conduct. It instructed soldiers to do everything possible to reduce civilian casualties. It also said that they should be well behaved and treat people properly in order to win them over. Allied leaders dismissed the code as propaganda.

The "new" Taliban made friends as well as money in the opium trade by protecting poppy farmers against U.S. forces. Troops trying to burn poppy crops were ambushed by the Taliban. Within a few years of the U.S. invasion, Afghan poppies provided more than 90 percent of the world's opium. U.S. commanders said the drug had become the Taliban's major economic support.

The Taliban also found support among other violent Islamic groups. Al Qaeda continued to send fighters to Afghanistan. Another Taliban ally known as the Haqqani Network was said to be more dangerous than the Taliban itself. The group nearly succeeded in assassinating President Hamid Karzai in 2008. The Haqqani Network was blamed for several deadly suicide bombings. The man believed to be its leader had commanded mujahideen in the war against the Soviets. The group also operated in Pakistan.

The Taliban Outside Afghanistan

As the Taliban grew stronger in Afghanistan, its influence also spread in the Pashtun areas of Pakistan. Madrassa teachers, businessmen, smugglers, and military officials in Pakistan had provided the Taliban with important aid in its early days. Pakistan's government denies giving direct support to the Taliban, but Western officials are sure that Pashtun officers in Pakistan's army and intelligence service secretly helped the Taliban over the years.

The government allowed the Taliban to rule in parts of Pakistan. Thousands of Pakistani girls were denied the right to go to school. Books, tapes, and videos were burned as they had been in Afghanistan. As the Taliban grew stronger and more aggressive, however, Pakistan's government began to worry. The Taliban was suspected

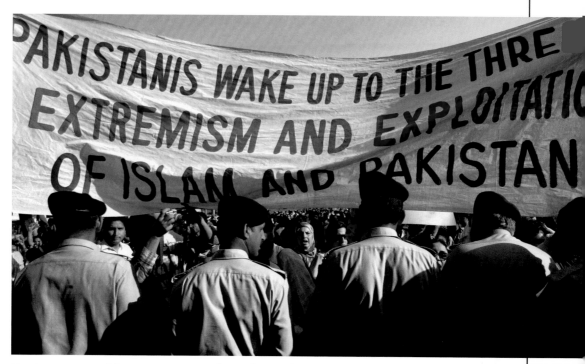

Protesters outside a mosque and madrassa in Islamabad, Pakistan's capital. Many Pakistanis became angry as the Taliban and similar groups outside Afghanistan tried to spread their ideas by force.

of carrying out terrorist attacks in Pakistan. U.S. officials urged Pakistan to take action. The United States began to attack Taliban targets inside Pakistan with remote-controlled drone aircraft. This enraged the Taliban, which accused the Pakistani government of cooperating with the United States. Taliban attacks increased.

In 2009, Pakistan began serious warfare against its Taliban groups. Strongholds were bombed, and soldiers on the ground occupied areas the Taliban had ruled. Hundreds of Taliban fighters were killed, including several important leaders.

While the Taliban has never aimed for control out-side of Afghanistan or Pakistan, it has inspired Islamic extremists in other countries. Gun battles have been reported in the central Asian countries of Uzbekistan, Tajikistan, and Kyrgyzstan. Human rights groups say governments in those countries have stifled dissent and religious freedom for fear of Taliban-style revolts. In faraway Nigeria, more than 150 people were killed in June 2009 when a group inspired by the Taliban went on a rampage.

Afghanistan's Future

In 2009, the United States began reducing its combat operations in Iraq, making more troops available for Afghanistan. But as the year drew to a close, more and more Americans were asking why the war should continue. There were more than one hundred thou-sand Western troops in Afghanistan, and sixty-eight thousand of them were Americans. Casualty rates were rising. The Taliban controlled much of Afghanistan outside the major cities.

Canada planned to withdraw its troops in 2011, and many people in Great Britain were calling for removal of their soldiers. Some Americans compared Afghanistan with Vietnam, where the United States fought a long and costly war that it was unable to win. They recalled an ominous name that Afghanistan had been given years earlier: Graveyard of Empires.

General Stanley A. McChrystal, the allied commander, said victory was possible. He ordered his troops to do more to protect the Afghan people, win their respect, and promote good government. However, many Afghans and outsiders saw the Afghan government as being hopelessly corrupt. The allies knew that the Afghan army and police could not stand up to the Taliban on their own.

A Taliban fighter surrenders to authorities in Pakistan. Pakistan began major military operations against its Taliban in 2009 after years of tolerating the radical group.

Taliban leaders said they were willing to talk about making peace but would never discuss it as long as foreign troops remained in Afghanistan. Taliban spokesmen said it didn't matter how many troops America sent—the Taliban would keep fighting.

Glossary

atheism The belief that there is no god.

Communism A political and social system that abolishes private ownership and calls for common ownership of property, land, and industry.

drone A small pilotless aircraft flown by remote control. U.S. forces used drones to attack Taliban and Al Qaeda targets in Afghanistan and Pakistan.

guerrilla A member of a small, irregular fighting force. Classic guerrilla tactics include sabotage, ambush, and hit-and-run attacks against larger forces.

hashish A drug that is common in Afghanistan.

improvised explosive device (IED) A handmade bomb that is set off by remote control.

International Security Assistance Force (ISAF) The military coalition headed by the United States that is responsible for security in Afghanistan.

Islam One of the world's great religions, founded by the prophet Muhammad. *Islam* is an Arabic word meaning "submission" or "surrender," meaning submission or surrender to God's will. Those who practice Islam are called Muslims.

jihad A holy struggle. Jihad may mean a war against enemies of Islam or it may mean a person's spiritual struggle to do the right thing.

madrassa An Islamic religious school.

mosque An Islamic house of worship. Muslims generally use the Arabic word *masjid*.

mujahideen A name that means "those who struggle," referring to people engaged in jihad. The mujahideen opposed the Soviet Union and the Soviet-backed Afghan government from 1979 to 1992.

mullah A teacher or interpreter of Islamic law. Mullahs are often the chief religious and legal authorities in small villages.

nongovernmental organization (NGO) Most NGOs are charities that collect money in wealthy countries and provide jobs, education, and services in poorer countries.

propaganda Information used to influence people's opinions. Propaganda can come in many forms, such as films, books, and flyers, and is often used by political organizations.

Qur'an The holy book of Islam; the collected teachings of the prophet Muhammad, revealed to him by God.

Soviet Union Officially, the Union of Soviet Socialist Republics. It was a Communist federation of European and Asian states dominated by Russia. The Soviet Union was established in 1922 and broke apart in 1991.

Taliban The Afghan version of an Arabic word meaning "students," particularly students in a religious school. One student is a *talib*.

For More Information

Afghanistan World Foundation
35 East 21st Street, 10th Floor
New York, NY 10010
(212) 228-3288
Web site: http://www.afghanistanworldfoundation.org
The Afghanistan World Foundation is dedicated to assisting reconstruction and development in Afghanistan. It promotes awareness of Afghans' struggles through events, media resources, and international partnerships.

Canadian Women for Women in Afghanistan
P.O. Box 86016
Marda Loop, Calgary AB T2T 6B7
Canada
(403) 244-5625
Web site: http://www.cw4wafghan.ca
The organization's goals are to advance education and educational opportunities for Afghan women and their families and to educate and increase the understanding of Canadians about human rights in Afghanistan.

Embassy of Afghanistan
2341 Wyoming Avenue NW
Washington, DC 20008

(202) 483-6410

Web site: http://www.embassyofafghanistan.org
Afghanistan's official representation in the United States provides information and services to Americans interested in doing business in Afghanistan or traveling to the country.

Embassy of Afghanistan in Canada
240 Argyle Avenue
Ottawa, ON K2P 1B9
Canada
(613) 563-4223
Web site: http://www.afghanemb-canada.net/en/
Afghanistan's official representation in Canada.

Web Sites

Due to the changing nature of Internet links, Rosen Publishing has developed an online list of Web sites related to the subject of this book. This site is updated regularly. Please use this link to access the list:

http://www.rosenlinks.com/itn/afgh

For Further Reading

Akhbar, Said Hyder, and Susan Burton. *Come Back to Afghanistan: A California Teenager's Story*. New York, NY: Bloomsbury USA, 2006.

Ali, Sharifa Enayat. *Afghanistan* (Cultures of the World). Tarrytown, NY: Marshall Cavendish Inc., 2008.

Barnes, Trevor. *Islam*. Boston, MA: Kingfisher Publications, 2005.

Doubleday, Veronica. *Three Women of Herat: A Memoir of Life, Love, and Friendship in Afghanistan*. London, England: Tauris Parke Paperbacks, 2006.

Gritzner, Jeffrey A., Charles F. Gritzner, and John F. Shroder. *Afghanistan*. New York, NY: Chelsea House Publishers, 2006.

Guibert, Emmanuel. *The Photographer: Into War-torn Afghanistan with Doctors Without Borders.* New York, NY: First Second, 2009.

Hafvenstein, Joel. *Opium Season: A Year on the Afghan Frontier*. Guilford, CT: Lyons Press, 2007.

Howard, Helen. *Living as a Refugee in America: Mohammed's Story*. Strongsville, OH: Gareth Stevens Publishing, 2005.

Jacobson, Sid, and Ernie Colon. *The 9/11 Report: A Graphic Adaptation*. New York, NY: Hill and Wang, 2006.

Khan, Rukhsana. *Wanting Mor.* Toronto, Canada: Groundwood Books, 2009.

Lunsford, Ralph. *The Taliban and Afghanistan.* Frederick, MD: PublishAmerica, 2009.

O'Brien, Tony, and Michael P. Sullivan. *Afghan Dreams: Young Voices From Afghanistan.* New York, NY: Bloomsbury USA, 2008.

Piddock, Charles. *Afghanistan.* Strongsville, OH: Gareth Stevens Publishing, 2006.

Staples, Suzanne Fisher. *Under the Persimmon Tree.* New York, NY: Douglas & McIntyre, Frances Foster Books, 2005.

Stewart, Gail B. *Life Under the Taliban.* Farmington Hills, MI: Cengage Gale, 2004.

Stine, Catherine. *Refugees.* New York, NY: Delacorte Press, 2005.

Van Der Gaag, Nikki. *Focus on Afghanistan.* Strongsville, OH: Gareth Stevens Publishing, 2007.

Wahab, Shaista, and Barry Youngerman. *A Brief History of Afghanistan.* New York, NY: Facts On File, 2007.

Whitehead, Kim. *Afghanistan.* Broomall, PA: Mason Crest Publishers, 2009.

Whitfield, Susan. *Countries of the World: Afghanistan.* Washington, DC: National Geographic Society, 2008.

Willis, Terry. *Afghanistan* (Enchantment of the World). Danbury, CT: Children's Press, 2008.

Bibliography

Bladauf, Scott, and Owais Tohid. "Taliban Appears to Be Regrouped and Well-funded." *Christian Science Monitor*, May 8, 2008. Retrieved August 1, 2009 (http://www.csmonitor.com/2003/0508/p01s02-wosc.html).

Blood, Peter R. "Afghanistan: A Country Study." Library of Congress. Retrieved September 2, 2009 (http://countrystudies.us/afghanistan/index.htm).

Burke, Jason. "The New Taliban." *Guardian*, October 14, 2007. Retrieved September 5, 2009 (http://www.guardian.co.uk/world/2007/oct/14/pakistan.afghanistan).

CNN.com. "Year-by-Year Highlights of War in Afghanistan." April 3, 2009. Retrieved August 22, 2009 (http://www.cnn.com/2009/WORLD/asiapcf/04/03/afghanistan.war.timeline/index.html).

Coll, Steve. *Ghost Wars: The Secret History of the CIA, Afghanistan, and bin Laden, from the Soviet Invasion to September 10, 2001*. New York, NY: Penguin Press, 2004.

The Cultural Orientation Project. "Afghans: Their History and Culture." June 30, 2002. Retrieved September 4, 2009 (http://www.cal.org/co/afghan/apeop.html).

Gwakh, Bashir Ahmad. "The Part-Time Taliban." Huffington Post. July 29, 2009. Retrieved July 30,

2009 (http://www.huffingtonpost.com/bashir-ahmad-gwakh/the-part-time-taliban_b_247503.html).

Hopkirk, Peter. *The Great Game: On Secret Service in High Asia*. Oxford, UK: Oxford University Press, 1990.

Ibrahimi, Sayed Yaqub. "Afghan Police Part of the Problem." Institute for War & Peace Reporting. June 1, 2006. Retrieved July 3, 2009 (http://iwpr.net/?o=321332&p=arr&s=f&apc_state=hena-police%20uniforms%20afghanistan_3_arr____publish_date_1_10_compact_11).

Kakar, Palwasha. "Tribal Law of Pashtunwali and Women's Legislative Authority." Islamic Legal Studies Program, Harvard University. Retrieved July 25, 2009 (http://www.law.harvard.edu/programs/ilsp/research/kakar.pdf).

Library of Congress, Federal Research Division. "Country Profiles: Afghanistan." August 2008. Retrieved September 5, 2009 (http://memory.loc.gov/frd/cs/profiles/Afghanistan.pdf).

NBC News. *Meet the Press*. Transcript for May 8, 2005. May 8, 2005. Retrieved August 13, 2009 (http://www.msnbc.msn.com/id/7761272).

PBS. "Analysis madrassas." *Frontline*. Retrieved September 5, 2009 (http://www.pbs.org/wgbh/pages/frontline/shows/saudi/analyses/madrassas.html).

Pennington, Rosemary. "The Five Pillars of Islam." Muslim Voices. January 1, 2009. Retrieved September 5, 2009 (http://muslimvoices.org/five-pillars-of-islam/).

Rashid, Ahmed. *Taliban*. New Haven, CT: Yale University Press, 2000.

Rhode, David, and David E. Sanger. "How a 'Good War' in Afghanistan Went Bad." *New York Times*, August 12, 2007. Retrieved August 23, 2009 (http://www.nytimes.com/2007/08/12/world/asia/12afghan.html?_r=2).

Robertson, Nic. "Afghan Taliban Spokesman: We Will Win the War." CNN. May 5, 2009. Retrieved August 31, 2009 (http://edition.cnn.com/2009/WORLD/asiapcf/05/04/robertson.interview.zabiullah.mujahid/index.html).

Smucker, Philip. "How Bin Laden Got Away." *Christian Science Monitor*, March 4, 2002. Retrieved September 4, 2009 (http://www.csmonitor.com/2002/0304/p01s03-wosc.html).

Thompson, Alex. "New Breed of Taliban Replaces Old Guard." *Telegraph*, September 16, 2008. Retrieved September 5, 2009 (http://www.telegraph.co.uk/news/worldnews/asia/afghanistan/2971811/New-breed-of-Taliban-replaces-old-guard.html).

Zerak, Fetrat. "The Occasional Taleban." Institute for War & Peace Reporting. April 23, 2009. Retrieved September 5, 2009 (http://www.iwpr.net/?p=arr&s=f&o=351992&apc_state=heniarr200904).

Index

About the Author

Larry Gerber has been a professional journalist for more than thirty years. He was in Afghanistan in 2005 as an adviser to Afghan journalists in a training program conducted by the Institute for War & Peace Reporting. He is a former Associated Press foreign correspondent and bureau chief.

Photo Credits

Cover (top left) Nathalie Behring-Chisholm/Getty Images; cover (top right) Robert Nickelsberg/Getty Images; cover (bottom), pp. 4, 10, 29 Roger Lemoyne/Getty Images; Roger Lemoyne/Getty Images; p. 6 Bildarchiv Preussischer Kulturbesitz/Art Resource, NY; p. 11 S. Sobolev/AFP/Getty Images; pp. 13, 14, 35, 46, 53 AFP/Getty Images; pp. 17, 22, 26 Per-Anders Pettersson/Getty Images; p. 19 Lourve, Paris, France/The Bridgeman Art Library (detail of illustrated page); p. 24 Emmanuel Dunand/AFP/Getty Images; pp. 30, 32 Stefan Smith/AFP/Getty Images; p. 34 Jean Claude-Chapon/AFP/Getty Images; pp. 38, 40 Mai/Time & Life Pictures/Getty Images; p. 41 Mario Tama/Getty Images; p. 43 Paula Bronstein/Getty Images; p. 45 Yoray Liberman/Getty Images; p. 47 Joe Raedle/Getty Images; p. 51 John Moore/Getty Images.

Designer: Tom Forget; Photo Researcher: Peter Tomlinson